Ways We Go

We Go on a
Subway

by Joanne Mattern

Red Chair Press   Egremont, Massachusetts

Look! Books are produced and published by Red Chair Press:

Red Chair Press LLC   PO Box 333   South Egremont, MA 01258-0333

www.redchairpress.com

 FREE Educator Guides at www.redchairpress.com/free-resources

Publisher's Cataloging-in-Publication Data
Names: Mattern, Joanne, 1963–
Title: We go on a subway / by Joanne Mattern.
Other Titles: Subway

Description: Egremont, Massachusetts : Red Chair Press, [2019] | Series:
    Look! books. Ways we go | Includes glossary and "Good to Know" fact
    boxes. | Interest age level: 004-007. | Includes bibliographical
    references and index. | Summary: "What to expect from a trip on a
    subway."--Provided by publisher.

Identifiers: ISBN 9781634406314 (library hardcover) | ISBN 9781634406437
    (paperback) | ISBN 9781634406376 (ebook) | LCCN 2018955664

Subjects: LCSH: Transportation--Juvenile literature. | Subways--Juvenile
    literature. | CYAC: Transportation. | Subways.

Classification: LCC HE152 .M385 2019 (print) | LCC HE152 (ebook) | DDC 388
    [E]--dc23

Photo credits: All iStock except for the following: pp. 8, 12–13, 16, 21
Shutterstock; pp. 9, 11, 17, 19 Alamy.

Printed in United States of America

0519 1P CGF19

Table of Contents

First Subway Ride

The subway is a train that runs underground. Subways take people all over the city. Let's see what it's like to ride on the subway.

Down in the Subway

Subways run in **tunnels** under the city streets. To get on the subway, you may have to go down stairs or ride an elevator.

59 St - Columbus Circle Station

Downtown 1

♿ Elevators at 8 Av & 58 St and across Broadway

Ⓐ Ⓒ Ⓑ Ⓓ & Uptown 1 via plat

7

Subway trains run on different lines. Each line goes to a different part of the city. Some cities use colors to name the lines. Other cities use numbers or letters.

In Boston, the subway lines are named for colors. This shows trains on the Red Line.

Paying for the Ride

You have to pay a **fare** to ride the subway. People buy a special card from a machine in the subway **station**.

People buy special cards to be able to ride a subway.

Next the person **swipes** the card at a **turnstile**. The turnstile lights up green. The person can go through now.

Here Comes the Train!

People wait for the train on a platform. An **announcer** says the train is coming. The train makes a big noise as it speeds into the station. Be sure to stand back until the train stops.

Riding the Train

Passengers sit or stand on the train. The train goes fast. The train is loud! It is dark outside the windows underground.

Getting Off the Subway

Here is your stop! It's time to get off the train. The doors open. People move quickly before the doors close.

The trains of a subway come and go quickly. But don't worry if you miss it. Another train will come soon.

To get to the street, you have to walk up stairs. Signs tell you where to go. You see light from the street. Then you walk outside. Your subway ride was fast, and lots of fun!

21

Words to Know

announcer: a person who gives information

fare: money you pay to ride a train or bus

passengers: people who travel in a vehicle

station: a stopping place for a train, subway, or bus

swipes: moves something sideways

tunnels: long underground passages

turnstile: a gate that turns to
let a person through

Learn More at the Library

Books (Check out these books to learn more.)

Clapper, Nikki Bruno. *City Trains.* Capstone Press, 2016.

Lassieur, Allison. *Subways in Action.* Capstone Press, 2012.

Leighton, Christina. *Subway Trains.* Bellwether Media, 2018.

Peters, Elisa. *Let's Ride the Subway.* PowerKids Press, 2015.

Index

About the Author

Joanne Mattern has written hundreds of nonfiction books for children. She likes writing about different people and places. Joanne lives in New York State with her family.